Vinolo

and his wooden children

Vivolo and His Wooden Children

Text and Photography
Ken Laffal

GALLERY PRESS   ESSEX   CONNECTICUT

Library of Congress Catalog Number 76-11492

ISBN 0-913622-04-4

Printed in the United States of America by
The Book Press, Brattleboro, Vermont 05301

Color separations and half-tones by Rendart,
Guilford, Connecticut 06437

Color printing by Beauvais Printing, Guilford,
Connecticut 06437

Contents

LIST OF ILLUSTRATIONS

FOREWORD

Vivolo and His Wooden Children describes a modern Connecticut folk artist and his work, by word and picture. One of Vivolo's carvings, *Man on a Chair*, occupies a prominent place in his family dining room. The figure sits with arms reaching out, beckoning his viewer to a warm embrace. The outstretched arms saying, "Come," are Vivolo's trademark. Photographer-writer Ken Laffal spent many hours with John Vivolo and his family in order to develop the detailed material for this sensitive, highly personal account of the artist. Laffal's photographs were carefully selected to show the range and verve of Vivolo's creativity.

In her Introduction, Florence H. Pettit relates Vivolo's work to the growing interest in twentieth century folk art. Laffal's text, which follows, is interspersed with pictures of Vivolo at work and photographs, some in color, of his pieces. There is a special section on Color, Form, and Theme in Vivolo's work by Florence Laffal, with additional photographs of Vivolo's pieces. Several of the pieces are given added commentary in order to call attention to interesting features. An Inventory and a Chronology of Vivolo's work, also by Florence Laffal, present by date, description, and current ownership, all of the artist's known work. The Inventory and Chronology offer student and collector alike, an immediate perspective on any particular piece.

John Vivolo's ninetieth birthday is on December 3, 1976. Despite his age, he devotes ten or more hours a day to his carving and painting. He has a sense of urgency, but he seems to grow stronger as he works. He has already made almost 200 significant pieces, yet under his hands a new host of wooden children is being born — weathervane whirligigs, musicians, and others. Along with the pieces pictured and described in this book, the new work of John Vivolo will become part of our twentieth century heritage of American folk art.

INTRODUCTION

The term *folk art* has come to be accepted in America as generally descriptive of drawings, paintings, carvings, and other objects made by hand by untutored and naive artisans depicting subjects taken from the life around them and their own beliefs and fantasies. In colonial America some of the objects familiar to everyone were ships' figureheads, cigar store Indians, weathervanes, whirligigs, eagles, wooden decoys, and farm and household implements. Most of these objects were made by people with professional standing as craft tradesmen and were produced in quantity. However, there was another large group of more or less ordinary people — farmers, sailors, housewives, laborers, wanderers — who worked at producing objects singly rather than in quantity, simply because they wanted to make something by hand. Sometimes the things made were utilitarian. They might, equally, have no specific use or only short-lived use; but they were invariably decorative and unique. Some of the more distinctive of these pieces were wood carvings of figures and animals, scrimshaw, dolls, Pennsylvania

German Fraktur paintings, embroidery, quilts, hooked rugs, and all kinds of toys and gadgets.

The work of all these American craftsmen and women echoed ancient craft traditions and continued the heritage of the European countries from which most of the settlers had come. Necessity dictated the making of many objects in the New World, but from the beginning there was a quality of inventiveness about American folk pieces, and though unpretentious, they had vigor and humor.

After the American Revolution the country proceded at a fast pace to establish her independence. New inventions set the wheels of industry turning, and agriculture became second in importance to manufacturing. Mass-production was the marvel of the age; there was less leisure time, and less will and almost no need to make things by hand. The court styles of France and England dictated a taste for more elegant artifacts. All during the march of industrial progress, some untaught artists continued carving, hammering, and stitching their individual objects, the audience and use for which was decidedly local.

American folk arts of the seventeenth, eighteenth, and nineteenth centuries did not attract much public interest until about 1925 when a few eastern museums assembled the first exhibitions, presenting the work not only as nostalgic and sometimes patriotic relics of early America, but as art. Collectors came to appreciate folk art for its simple and often unique concepts that showed ignorance of or complete disdain for the "rules" of more formal art. These pieces had a decided straightforwardness that was unusual and refreshing at a time when sophisticated art was becoming more esoteric. American folk arts are today of great interest to a growing number of people; they are a distinctive part of American culture.

The most recent development is the recognition that folk art is not only an expression of earlier centuries, but is a continuing part of the life of twentieth century American men and women who follow an independent vision, held to strongly despite the modern bombardment of complex influences on mind, eye and ear.

These contemporary folk artists seem to be very little different from folk artists in previous times. They express themselves by making all sorts of objects ranging from Simon Rodia's lacy towers of cement in Los Angeles and roadside sculpture along the highways of the west, to primitive religious carvings made in Missouri and paintings of a throbbing metropolis done in a Brooklyn apartment. They make use of modern materials, but their work has the same intrinsic qualities as pieces produced in the more serene days of early America. Herbert W. Hemphill, Jr., collector and lover of American folk art says, in his book, *Twentieth-Century American Folk Art and Artists,* "In presenting their visions without consideration of accepted theory or rules, their art is a splendid testament to the innate creativity present and recurring spontaneously in every generation — and even within us, the viewers, if we will but restore our intuitive perception."

The sort of perception one must have to recognize the values in folk art is more elusive than we might think. It is easy to see that a work is technically unskilled, or that there is a puzzling eccentricity about it. A viewer may try to apply obvious criteria to a simple carving: "The head is too big; the arms are too short." Such academic standards can never be made to fit the inventions of a folk artist who draws from a private vision expressed only in his work. The folk artist is a rarity — an uninhibited person whose creations, sometimes wryly witty, are his alone. Some viewers may feel that such an arbitrary approach cannot possibly produce art.

Other viewers may see that folk art is original and highly inventive; they are pleased by an execution that is delightfully free, whether it is full of expressive details or almost devoid of them. People who are charmed by untutored art are apt to say, "I love that carving." Their feeling is expressed by the word *love*, and this spontaneous reaction to work that possesses an intensely human quality may be the key to its power.

Hemphill's graceful evaluation of folk art and of ourselves as viewers is as succinct as one could hope to find. The picture fits wood-carver John Vivolo as neatly as do the suits painted on his carved figures. This energetic, warm-hearted man who had no formal education has been influenced by what he has seen and by what life itself has taught him, but to his experience he has also brought a vivid imagination. Vivolo's subjects are people we know — the solid-looking man we saw yesterday peering into a store window, the rock singer in the movies, the hero astronaut on T.V., but his birds, his castles, and even his windmills have a touch of the unreal.

Vivolo takes patriarchal pride in his carvings. He calls them "all my wooden children," and he has indeed fathered something from within himself that, until old age and retirement gave him freedom from grueling daily work, he did not even know he was nurturing. It is the warmth of the man himself and an artist's eye guiding the hands of a natural craftsman that join with an inner vision to give Vivolo's work its charm and its unquestionable validity as twentieth century folk art.

Florence H. Pettit
Glenbrook, Connecticut

BEGINNINGS

John Vivolo took a long drag on his pipe. "I'll tell you," he said, gesturing toward the heavens, "I got tired of sitting around waiting for them to come and get me. I had to do something to keep myself busy. That's why I started carving." He began without the faintest idea of becoming something called an artist.

The year was 1957 and Vivolo was feeling restless. It had only been a few months since he had retired, but even at the age of seventy-one, he felt cramped by inac-

1. Lighting up.

17

tivity. He had to make something, he had to use his hands. One day he picked up his hammer and chisel, and began hacking away at a dried log which had been lying in the cellar. Out of the smooth surface of the wood a body emerged, then a face began to appear. Vivolo became excited. In a frenzy of activity, he lost track of time. Day passed into night, and still he carved. It was not until early morning that the hammering ceased. Exhaustion had overtaken him. Covered with wood chips, he fell into a restless sleep on the sofa. An army of wooden men marched through his dreams, and he awoke with a start, feeling he had slept for hours. Seeing the carved figure, he ran his hand over it, and knew that he had created something living out of a piece of throwaway wood. He switched on the light over his workbench to get a better look, and saw that the piece lacked something. It needed color, lots of color. He opened several cans of latex paint and went to work. A couple of days and many layers of paint later, he was finished.

Feeling initially that the carving had "turned out pretty good," Vivolo soon became distracted by the length of its nose. It did not fit his mental picture of the "perfect face." At once he started a second piece. Soon more and more logs originally destined for the fireplace began appearing in his work space.

A man of few words, Vivolo pursued his new occupation with a passion. Living and working had always been one and the same for him, and his carving was no exception. He became totally committed to it, and in the nineteen years since the first piece was created, a veritable mountain of sawdust and wood chips fell under his prolific saw and chisel.

"Working gives me strength," says Vivolo, and it is his seemingly inexhaustible energy which is the most striking characteristic of this eighty-nine year old man. He is

2. Inspecting a log.

an intense man, capable of utmost concentration on the task at hand. His eyes sparkle youthfully and his relatively unlined face breaks easily into a smile. Speaking slowly, his husky voice betraying a slight Italian accent, he often livens up his stories with colorful Italian expressions. His large, rough hands and broad shoulders tell of years of strenuous labor. Yet, unfailingly and with great dignity, he is to be found wearing tie, and often fedora, even while working.

The physical endurance built up during six decades of manual labor enables him to carve for up to twelve hours a day, pausing only to eat and to rest briefly. He has remained free of the ills of old age, and his imagination is as vivid as a child's. The years seem to have increased his energy, and his productivity amazes those around him.

3. First cut.

He has become quite proficient at his art, and a carving which once took weeks is now finished in days.

In his tight work space, Vivolo usually has five or six pieces in varying stages of completion. Arms are sanded, hats fitted, hair and mustaches glued, and shoes painted, in a whirlwind of activity which assures the continuous emergence of new pieces. He shrugs off any suggestion of moderating his schedule. "I've got a job to do. If I don't do it, who will?" He feels a deep commitment to the wooden children, not only to those which now fill his house, but even more to those which crowd his imagination, waiting to become reality.

When he talks of future projects, though, Vivolo is cautious, prefacing his remarks with, "If I have time." According to his son Frank, Vivolo has been saying this for the past twenty-five years. Yet in watching him work, one can sense the increasing urgency that he feels. He knows that he can not go on defying Father Time, so he lives as fully as he knows how: by expressing himself intensely in his work.

Vivolo was born in 1886 in the southern Italian village of Accri. Accri was a closely knit rural community where friends were easily made and often kept for a lifetime. Like most of the men in the village, Vivolo's father was an impoverished farm laborer, employed by one of the wealthy, land-owning "paisans." Day in, day out, the men worked the land, as their fathers and grandfathers had done for generations before them. Their harvest was bountiful, but their wages remained a pittance, hardly enough to keep a family alive.

Even though Vivolo was too young to follow his father to the fields, his time was not spent in childhood play. His mother had numerous kitchen chores for him,

4. In process, *Male-Female Band*, 1976.

and his father entrusted him with responsibility for tending the family livestock. When he was eight, Vivolo's father sent him out to help in the wheat fields.

The Mediterranean sun was strong, and although Vivolo earned only a few cents a day, he was happy with his new job in the warm, golden fields. Being the youngest in his work crew, he was given the lighter tasks, such as picking up the loose grain which had fallen beside the reaping machine. He was, however, soon to find out that being the smallest was not always an advantage. One day, during the height of the harvest, the reaper stopped working. Quickly looking over his crew, the boss singled

5. Rasping.

out Vivolo to pick up a part which had fallen under the belt of the malfunctioning machine. Vivolo had just gotten down to retrieve the part, when suddenly the belt began to rotate again, cutting deeply into his forehead. "Another couple of inches," says Vivolo, pointing to a long scar, "and this would have been two heads." He was treated by a local doctor and was back to work within forty-eight hours.

But his days in Accri were numbered. His parents spoke to him of America, where a man who was willing to work could earn a fine living. Vivolo understood quite well that he could not hope to raise himself out of

6. Sawing.

poverty on the meager wages of a farm laborer in Accri, and he dreamed of what it would be like to be rich and to have a house, perhaps even a farm of his own. He knew then that some day he would go to the "land of money" across the sea. That "some day" came sooner than Vivolo imagined, for he was only fourteen when his parents announced that they had accumulated enough money to pay for his passage. And so in 1900, John Vivolo, armed with little else than two good hands and a strong back, left the quiet security of his native village and headed toward Naples and an uncertain future.

He completed the first leg of his journey by train. It took the entire day to travel the 150 mile distance from Accri to the port city, but Vivolo was not in a hurry. Not wishing to take any chances, he had started a full day early. As soon as the train arrived in busy Naples, Vivolo went down to the harbor and settled himself in a corner of the loading dock. By nightfall many more people had assembled on the dock. Vivolo fell asleep, and when he awoke early in the morning, the area was swarming with people. Every foot of available space was jammed with bags, boxes, and parcels, and he himself was tightly wedged between two huge hatboxes and a crate of oranges.

As the hour drew near for the departure of the trans-Atlantic steamer, the main dock became a scene of increasing chaos. Women cried over the imminent separation from their loved ones, boat workers cursed the overweight baggage, vendors hawked American flags and Italian snacks, and customs officials ran nervously back and forth, checking tickets and immigration papers. Vivolo himself was too excited to pay much attention to the activity around him. Three days earlier, when he had taken sad

7. Chiseling.

leave of his family, his mother had wept, despite his assurances that he would return as soon as he had saved up enough money. But now, surrounded by thousands of unfamiliar faces, Vivolo felt that his family was already far away. He became impatient, waiting amidst the turmoil. Finally the horn blew, and the ramp gate was opened. Clutching his vital documents in one hand and his overstuffed cloth satchel in the other,

8. Vivolo and one of his favorite pieces. (See ill. 27)

Vivolo boarded the ship and took his place on the deck. This would be his home for the next eighteen days.

As the coast of Italy disappeared beyond the horizon, he broke open the first of many food parcels that his mother had packed for him. Soon the gentle swaying of the steamer changed to violent rocking, and hundreds of green-faced passengers staggered toward the railings. Vivolo himself was blessed with an iron stomach, and the severe pitching did nothing to daunt his appetite. Throughout the journey a series of storms kept the majority of the travelers glued to the railing. Not Vivolo. He finished his homemade rations within a week, and then became one of the few passengers who regularly availed themselves of the ship's dining facilities. The eighteen days passed quickly for Vivolo, and early one morning the ship passed the mist-enshrouded Statue of Liberty and entered New York harbor.

At disembarkation, Vivolo was met by a cousin who had sponsored his trip to the United States. Sponsors were supposed to guarantee to the authorities that the immigrant would have a place to stay, as well as a job. Those who arrived without such sponsorship were not even allowed to leave the boat. Not knowing a word of English, and awed by the ocean of humanity around him, Vivolo was more than happy to entrust himself to his seemingly all-knowing cousin. Together they left for West Virginia, where his cousin was employed as a miner. Upon arrival at the workcamp, Vivolo was shown to his bunk and given his coal mining tools. Later he learned that his bed and tools had belonged to another miner who had been killed the day before Vivolo's arrival when a misplaced explosive buried him under an avalanche of coal.

Vivolo knew nothing about explosives, but learned quickly. He developed a knack for placing his dynamite in areas where the most coal would be loosened, with the least possible danger to himself. Dynamiting was only the initial step, however, for the miners were paid by the amount of coal shoveled into their carts. The carts held five tons of coal each, and the pay was ten cents per cart.

9. Painting a whirligig.

Out of this munificent wage they had to purchase their own dynamite, as well as the shovels and pickaxes for their work. The company provided food and a bunk.

On a good day Vivolo could loosen and shovel twenty tons of coal. The company did not limit the number of hours that the miners could work each day, so their earnings depended strictly on their own initiative. Vivolo often extended his working day to ten or twelve hours, for he wanted to save up as much money as possible. Every month he would send some of his hard earned dollars back to his family in Italy.

10. *Sawing Wood Weathervane Whirligig*, 1975, 19"x46".

There was little to do in the camp, other than work, and most of the miners took only Sunday as a day of rest. As they relaxed from the week of hard labor, the men were accosted by a local minister who tried to persuade them to spend their free time in more godly pursuits. Few of the miners responded to his overtures. Nevertheless, he persisted every week in his search for converts. Finally, one Sunday, Vivolo and his cousin decided to pay the minister's church a visit. The service was short, and the inevitable collection plate soon began its rounds. When it came to the two young visitors, they reached reluctantly into their pockets. Vivolo's cousin dropped a ten cent coin onto the plate, but Vivolo had only a five dollar bill in his pocket. He laid the bill, the equivalent of two weeks' work, beside the coin, and waited anxiously for his change. On seeing the bill, the minister's face lit up and he took Vivolo's hand. "God bless you, my son," he said.

Vivolo could not understand the English words, but the pious look in the minister's eyes was unmistakable. He glanced at his cousin for help, but the minister's blessings were so profuse that the cousin dared not ask for a refund. Who were they to argue with a man of the cloth? In any case, Vivolo finally told himself philosophically, he might well be blessed with eternal sanctity for his magnanimous gift, and that would certainly make the investment worthwhile. Vivolo filled his subsequent Sundays with such earthly pursuits as sleeping and playing ball with his fellow workers.

Vivolo and his cousin worked at the West Virginia mine for three years. When word spread through the camp of a better paying job opportunity in Maryland, they packed their bags and headed north. The new project was railroad construction, and the first task of the laborers was to dig out the bed in which the track would eventually be laid. Vivolo and his cousin were assigned to a work crew of non-English speaking Italians. The workers themselves had no part in negotiating the contract under which they were hired, and since they could not speak English, they were forced to place their collective fate in the hands of their foreman.

Vivolo was worried. The pay seemed good, but the living conditions were severe. At the turn of the century, work crew labor was in many respects close to slavery. Once a company had contracted a laborer, they meant to keep him. The men were housed in a fenced-in, prison-like community. The company provided everything, including the store from which the workers had to buy all their supplies. Prices were exorbitant, and as a result, it was almost impossible to save anything out of one's wages. The

11. *Meeting*, 1973, 7" to 8".

men were not at liberty to leave, and there were armed watchmen to make sure that no one tried. As time went on, Vivolo became obsessed with one thought — to escape. But day and night, the watchmen kept their eyes on the work crews. It so happened, however, that on Easter Sunday, a work holiday, Vivolo and four of his friends were allowed to play ball outside the company fences. It was now or never. Gradually, they threw the ball further and further until they reached the banks of a small river. Here, out of earshot of the watchmen, they called across the water to a farmhouse on the opposite side and offered the farmer two cents to row them across the fifty foot stretch of water. He agreed and did so. It was a small price to pay for freedom!

Having only the clothes he was wearing and fifteen dollars in his pocket, Vivolo walked the few miles back to Baltimore. There, parting company with his cousin, he took a train to New York City. He had the Manhattan address of an older couple who had known his parents in the old country, and he set out to find them. He himself could not read the address on the crumpled piece of paper he had carefully preserved in his wallet, so he enlisted the help of a passerby. Through the seemingly end-

12. *Two Lantern Men*: 1961, 11"; 1975, 36".

less streets, Vivolo found his way to the teeming markets of the Lower East Side. As he passed along the pushcarts loaded with food, clothing, and every other imaginable item, Vivolo heard snatches of Italian among the many languages being spoken. When he finally arrived at the brown brick tenement, though, his heart was suddenly filled with fear. What if they did not live here anymore, or even worse, what if they did but refused to help him? He had no other refuge in this frighteningly complex and confusing city. His fears were, however, quickly assuaged, when a heavyset Italian woman opened the door. Upon hearing his name, she threw her arms around him, brought him inside, and within minutes had set a large plate of steaming spaghetti before him. It was the first homemade meal he had eaten in years, and Vivolo cherished every bite. His host eagerly asked him about affairs in Accri, and though his "news" was about three and a half years old, she listened with rapt attention. When her husband came home from work, they talked until late into the night, but before going to bed, Vivolo's hosts assured him that he could stay with them.

One morning, as Vivolo walked through the market, he was approached by a stranger who addressed him in

13. *Wonder Woman*, 1966, 12". Courtesy Mr. M. Tsangaris.

his native tongue. "You look like a strong young man, do you want a job?" Vivolo nodded eagerly. The man owned a bakery, and he needed someone immediately. He promised Vivolo a substantial wage, two meals a day, and a place to sleep in the bakery, in return for his services as a delivery boy. Accustomed to shoveling tons of coal or earth for a few pennies wage, Vivolo could not imagine why anyone would offer so much for mere delivery work. He had seen hundreds of pushcarts in the neighborhood, handled easily by boys little more than half his age. As he took leave of the older couple who had given him shelter, Vivolo told them how lucky he had been to encounter such a generous boss.

When he arrived at the bakery at seven o'clock in the morning, the streets were already beginning to come alive with delivery boys and their carts. Vivolo was eager to get started, but when he saw his own cart, his spirits sank. This was no ordinary pushcart. Rather, it was more like a wagon, and as he maneuvered the clumsy vehicle onto the street, Vivolo wondered whether he might not actually be replacing a horse. His route took him along Houston Street to the intersection of Mott Street, and then through a maze of side streets below

14. *Cowboy on Oak Horse,*
1958, 18".

Houston. By four o'clock in the afternoon his entire body ached. It was not until evening that Vivolo finally returned the empty wagon to the bakery. He was in a state of physical exhaustion. That night, at dinner, the boss's wife asked him if he had enjoyed his first day of work. Her eyes showed only kindness, and Vivolo dared not look at her. "It was O.K.," he mumbled, quickly filling his mouth with food. How could he tell them the truth, that he hated the work, that he had cursed the fresh loaves of bread every step of the way.

"Was the wagon not too heavy?" asked the boss.

Vivolo felt uncomfortable. He knew that they were concerned only with his well-being, yet the questions were embarrassing. He wanted to tell them the truth, but as he sat in their home and enjoyed a second helping of home cooked food, he knew that he could not be honest with them.

"No, it was not too heavy, I was able to handle it," he responded.

For the next two weeks Vivolo suffered. At the age of eighteen he was too proud to concede that he was unable to perform the strenuous task. But every day seemed longer, and the pain in his muscles was unbear-

15. *Pasta Eater*, 1971, 21½".
Courtesy Mr. M. Tsangaris.

able. He was simply not strong enough for the job. As he became increasingly worn down by the work, the boss became more and more friendly. Vivolo was outfitted with new clothing, given extra spending money for the weekend, and treated like a member of the boss's family.

Finally, one afternoon, Vivolo could no longer stand the strain. As he pulled the wagon into the alley next to the bakery, he noticed that everyone had gone home for the evening. He gathered all his belongings, tied them into a bundle, and walked out into the market. He knew that dinner would be waiting for him at the boss's house, but he dared not go there. He was ashamed. He had been given a job to do, and he had failed. After two weeks, he was already giving up.

Vivolo passed the boss's house that evening, but he did not stop to say goodbye. Instead, he returned to the house of his parents' friends, and explained what had happened. The old man knew of a job opening, but Vivolo would have to leave New York City and travel north. Vivolo felt no particular attachment to the city, and was glad to get as far away as possible from his Lower East Side bakery. That same night he boarded a train for Buffalo.

16. Detail, *Pasta Eater.*

The address which he had been given was that of
a large butcher shop. The owner knew Vivolo's hosts in
New York City, and was happy to give him a job. In
early 1900, canning and freezing were unknown, and
meat was dipped in a kind of starch to keep it fresh.
The task of preserving the meat in this way was delegated
to Vivolo. His job was simple and repetitive but the lack
of physical exertion appealed to him. He decided that this
was definitely a job worth holding on to, offering as it
did, a chance to save money with a minimum of effort.

As the roll of bills in his shirt became thicker, Vivolo's thoughts turned to the old country. Soon he would
have enough money to afford the trip, and he began to
long for Accri. Two and a half years at the butcher shop
were enough for him to save the necessary two hundred
dollars for the journey back to Italy.

THE MAN

In New York, as he boarded the oceangoing liner,
Vivolo felt the same excitement he had known six years
earlier on the distant shore. He was returning to Italy
as a real "paisan," with money in his pocket. He was

17. *Standing Mustached Man,*
1976, 29½".

twenty years old, an extremely eligible bachelor. In Accri, the village girls talked of him with considerable interest, and a friend of his brother suggested that Vivolo come over to his parents' farm to meet his sister. The meeting was arranged, and the two were attracted to each other immediately. Vivolo decided to stay on the farm to work, and within a year they were married. But farm life in Accri had little future, and a short time after their marriage the couple left Accri for America.

When he returned to the States in 1907, Vivolo found work with a Hartford, Connecticut construction company. He and his wife went to live in a tiny apartment in the city, but the year in Accri had rekindled his love of the earth, and now he was impatient to have a piece of land of his own. By 1910 he had saved enough money to purchase several 25 x 100 foot plots of land in the Columbia Gardens section of Hartford. Located along the Connecticut River in what is now an industrial park a few miles south of downtown Hartford, Columbia Gardens was then a sparsely populated residential area. There were about fifteen other families living in the vicinity when Vivolo began building his own wood frame house. His son Paul described the house raising.

18. *Lamb Dog*, 1971, 13½".
Courtesy Mr. M. Tsangaris.

"In the old days, everyone helped each other out. If somebody wanted to build something, and he needed a hand, he'd call all the paisans, you know, all his friends and cousins, maybe buy them a few cases of beer, a little wine, plenty of spaghetti and things to eat. And they'd all get together and work. My father did the same thing. That's how he got his house built."

In the final stages of construction, however, misfortune befell Vivolo. A lighted match was accidentally thrown, and the entire structure burned to the ground. Not a man to resign himself to fate, Vivolo borrowed money from a cousin and immediately began work on a second house. However, he was not planning to take any more chances with fire. He second house was constructed entirely of brick and mortar, with steel beams. The building was completed in 1916, and Vivolo proudly moved his wife, then pregnant, out of the tiny Hartford apartment, into their spacious new quarters.

Ever since Vivolo was a young boy in Accri he had loved animals and had longed for the day when he could have a farm of his own. Finally a landowner, he eagerly made plans for husbandry. He would need chicken coops, rabbit cages, pigeon houses, a pig pen, and a large barn.

19. *Chicken Slaughter Weathervane Whirligig*, 1966, 20"x17"x 15½". Courtesy Kelter-Malce. (See ill. 56)

He spent every available hour in the evenings and on weekends preparing for the arrival of his animals. The smaller outbuildings he built by himself, and when he needed help with the barn, he enlisted the aid of his friends and relatives with a huge wine and pasta barn-raising party. It took several of these gatherings to complete the job, but eventually the two-story barn was ready.

There was a weekly animal market in Hartford, and it was here that Vivolo made his first purchase, a milking cow named "Rosie." Vivolo immediately fell in love with Rosie, and every morning before pedaling off to work on his bicycle, he would milk her and lead her out to pasture. There, in the open meadowland surrounding Vivolo's property, Rosie could graze to her heart's content. One cow did not fulfill his dream of a farm, however, and soon several sheep were added to keep Rosie company. Even in those days a family could enjoy substantial savings in their food budget by raising their own meat and eggs, so Vivolo expanded his livestock to include chickens, ducks, geese, rabbits, pigs, and pigeons.

Vivolo became a true farmer, with that uncanny ability to be personally close to his animals in the spring, yet able, when the time came in the fall, to slaughter

20. *Man on White-tailed Chicken*, 1974, 18".

them. There were other families in the neighborhood who also raised animals for meat, but it was always Vivolo who was called upon to perform the butchering task. Small in stature, Vivolo seemed an unlikely candidate for a life and death struggle with a frightened, squealing four hundred pound pig, yet the outcome was never in doubt.

On special occasions, such as Easter, Vivolo would slaughter one of his sheep and invite the whole neighborhood to his house to join in the celebration. His wife prepared a bountiful feast, and the tables were piled high with fresh meat and homegrown vegetables. Wine flowed freely, and spirits were high. The Vivolos rejoiced in the warmth of their friends' companionship. Even when Vivolo's young family became larger, he still cherished company and always welcomed visitors with open arms.

In the first years at Columbia Gardens, Vivolo turned his energies toward the practical task of improving the living conditions of his expanding family. Soon after moving into his new home, he was confronted with a problem involving the water supply. The city was unwilling to provide water for the thinly populated Columbia Gardens, so he decided to take matters into his own

21. *Devil*, 1969, 14''. Courtesy Mr. M. Tsangaris.

hands. He began digging, and since his land was somewhat swampy, he did not have to dig very far before finding water. However, the idea of having to go outside to a pump, did not appeal to him. Some of the larger farms in the area had irrigation windmills, and he was certain he could put such a structure to work for his own benefit. He drove several twenty foot wooden beams into the earth and hoisted a huge five hundred gallon wood barrel up to the top of the trestle. The windmill sails were completed with scrap tin and discarded piping which he had brought home from his construction site. Never having built such a contraption before, Vivolo was delighted when the wind began to turn the sails, and the tank began to fill with water drawn from the well. Stopping the process was another matter, though, and when the wind suddenly began to "blow like hell," Vivolo was forced to run for cover from the overflowing water, raining down from twenty feet above. The solution turned out to be fairly simple for, with a wooden pole, he could block the blades of the rotary sail at will. The gawky windmill became a landmark of Columbia Gardens. Not only eye-catching, but practical as well, it provided water for central heating, the kitchen tap, and a flush toilet.

22. *Astronaut*, 1971, 13".

Vivolo's family was thus the first in Columbia Gardens to enjoy these modern conveniences.

As time went by, Vivolo became even more enterprising. His house was not yet connected to the electrical power lines, but he decided to prepare for the day when it would be. His children would soon be going to school, and the kerosine lamps now used by the family would simply not serve. With the help of a friend, Vivolo wired his house from top to bottom. For the next twenty years he sent request after request to the electric company, but was steadfastly denied service. The company was not interested in a total of one or two customers in Columbia Gardens.

Vivolo and his wife both wanted a big family, and by 1930 their seventh child was born. Vivolo worked overtime, often until late in the night, to provide for his family. During the days of the Depression he watched his earnings eaten up by necessary items which he could no longer afford. In these hard times his wife was a constant source of help and support. But later that year she fell ill with tuberculosis.

No single event brought the family as close together as her death in 1931. Paul, the oldest son, recalls:

23. *Cowboy on Horse*, 1974, 18''.

"I was fifteen when my mother died. The city of Hartford wanted to take and split the family up. But my father wouldn't let that happen. 'Never,' he said. 'They can never split our family.' But the city tried. They came and took my sister and my youngest brother and put them into the Children's Village, an orphanage. But they weren't even there for a week. My father couldn't stand it. He missed them so much that he went and got them back."

The burden of being a widower with seven young children was overwhelming. Vivolo took on extra masonry work on the weekends, to supplement his meager earnings as a construction worker. Even with with this added income, there was barely enough for food, clothing, and other necessities of a growing family. The children helped

24. *LBJ*, 1968, 14".

25. Detail, *LBJ*. Courtesy Mr. M. Tsangaris.

58

but Vivolo was forced to spend what little spare time he had, cooking, sewing, maintaining the house, and even shoe-making.

Although his financial outlook was bleak, Vivolo never sought help from anyone. He worked at countless jobs in the construction industry, and whenever a better paying, even risky, job opportunity presented itself, he was there. His tasks ranged from carpentry and painting to bricklaying and roadbuilding, but his specialty was demolition work. For years he drove off to work each morning in a dilapidated Ford filled with live explosives. By showing a consistent willingness to undertake the most difficult and dangerous jobs, Vivolo became popular with bosses. He had developed a reputation as a "company man," a worker who followed every order explicitly, and who always completed his jobs on time. This reputation was crucial to his family's survival during the Depression. When men lined up for the few jobs available, only the hardest workers, like Vivolo, were chosen. He rarely missed a day at work. If a project had to be completed during the lunch break, he would skip lunch. He never complained, he kept his feelings to himself, and he studiously avoided trouble. Although he was one of the

26. *Production Boss*, 1958, 16".

smallest men in his work crew, few could match his output. His son Frank had this to say about his father:

"He was a hard worker. He didn't know how to work normally. He was always like three men. No matter how tired he got, he'd never show it. I once had a job here in Bloomfield, and my father came along to help. He must have been about seventy years old then. We dropped about twelve or fourteen loads of soil for an area that had to be planted. I went away for two or three hours to take care of some other business, and when I got back, my dad had all that soil spread out. Normally we would have hired a crew to do that, but he went and did the whole job himself."

As his children grew older, Vivolo began to delegate the household tasks to them. The girls took over the sewing and cleaning, and looked after the younger children, while the boys tended the animals and kept a constant supply of wood on hand for the furnace. According to the oldest daughter Jeannie, it was Vivolo who taught her the intricacies of preparing Italian delicacies, and even today Vivolo will sometimes cook for his family. The boys showed little culinary interest, but spent hours tinkering with Model-T Fords salvaged at the motor vehicle dump.

27. *Man on a Chair*, 1975, 36". (See III. 8)

27. *Man on a Chair*, 1975, 36''. (See Ill. 8)

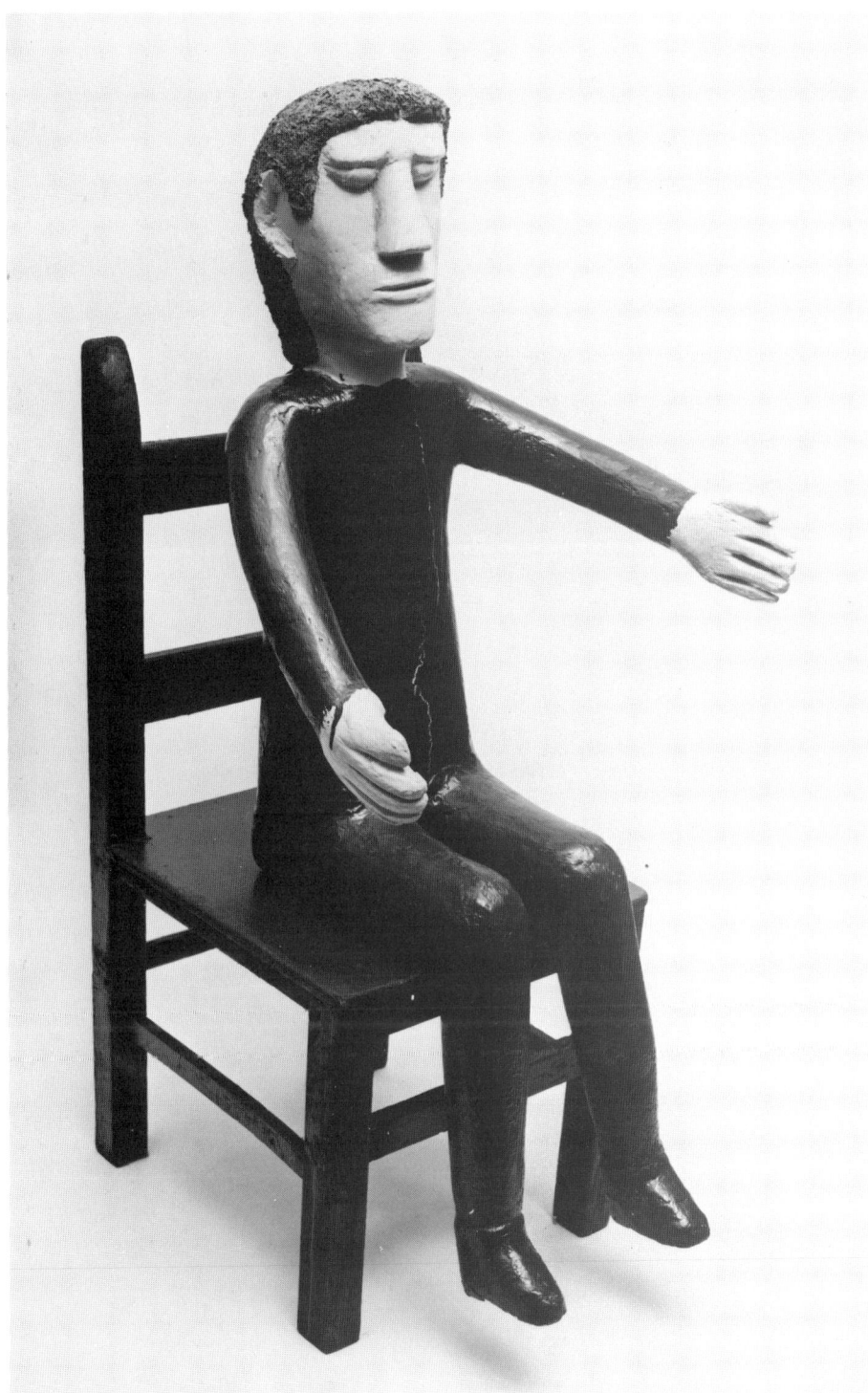

COLOR ILLUSTRATIONS

28. Vivolo and his wooden children. Front row left: three men from *Meeting*, 1973 (ill. 11) and *Two Goats*, 1958 (ill. 38). Second row, left to right: *Guitar Player*, 1970 (ill. 40); *Standing Man*, 1972 (inv. 131); *Nutcracker Man*, 1963 (ill. 59); *Candle Man*, 1970 (ill. 60); *Rock Star*, 1973 (ill. 51); *Astronaut*, 1971 (ill. 22). Back row, left to right: *Standing Man*, 1976 (inv. 141); John Vivolo; *Standing Mustached Man*, 1976 (ill. 17).

29. *Man on Black Chicken*, 1974, 18″. Courtesy Mr. & Mrs. J. Laffal, Essex, Conn. (Cover illustration).

30. *Band*, 1969, 16½″ to 18″. Courtesy Mr. M. Tsangaris, New York (See ill. 42, 47, 53).

31. *Three Birds*, 1971, 1972, 1973, 6″, 7″, and 7″.

32. *Woodsman Weathervane Whirligig*, 1967, 38″x37″. Courtesy Mr. & Mrs. J. Laffal, Essex, Conn. (See ill. 57, 61, 62).

33. *Barbershop Trio*, 1973, 15″.

34. *Nutcracker Man*, 1976, 20″.

35. *Flag Weathervane Whirligig*, 1975, 31″x44″ (See ill. 36, 65).

28. Vivolo and his wooden children.

29. *Man on Black Chicken.*

30. *Band.*

31. *Three Birds.*

32. *Woodsman Weathervane Whirligig.*

33. *Barbershop Trio.*

34. *Nutcracker Man.*

35. *Flag Weathervane Whirligig.*

36. Detail, opposite page.

To earn money, the boys rebuilt engines, using parts from the motors of the discarded cars. One of the old cars, stripped down to the chassis, drove a saw for cutting firewood. Each of the older boys had a car of his own, but times were still bad and the family income could not support fuel for joyriding. One day Paul, the oldest boy, taking a shortcut to school, noticed a drip at the tap of a Standard Oil storage tank. Dismayed by the waste, he was struck by an idea. That night he returned with a five gallon can and a funnel, which he placed under the tap. Early next morning the can was overflowing with gas. He had found a supplier. Ingenuity and effort were called for from everyone. For her part, Jeannie, the oldest daughter, ran her heart out for three days each summer at Colt's Park in Hartford, where the city held its annual races for local teenagers. Her overwhelming desire to win made her just a little faster than her competitors. It was not the glory of winning, however, that propelled her to victory summer after summer, but the twenty pound sack of flour offered to the runner who finished first.

Flooding was a predictable springtime occurrence in the low lying meadowlands of Columbia Gardens, and Vivolo had learned to cope with it. Depending on the

37. *Gold Lady*, 1973, 14½".

amount of snow which had fallen during the winter, Vivolo was faced with either a minor inconvenience or a major disaster. During all his twenty years at Columbia Gardens, though, he had never experienced anything !ike the flood of 1936. That spring the water kept rising, and Vivolo was forced to move his family to his sister's apartment in Hartford. His barn was located in a particularly low area, and he worried that his livestock might drown. In a mass animal movement reminiscent of Noah, Vivolo transported all his animals, via a seventy-five foot ramp, to the second story of his barn. There, he and his son Paul built a "Noah's Ark" raft out of old railroad ties, and drove the animals onto this buoyant platform. As the water rose, so did the raft with the cow, the sheep, the pigs, and smaller animals. Fortunately the water subsided as the cow was bumping her head against the roof.

After a few weeks Vivolo was ready to return to Columbia Gardens to begin repairing his house and barn. But the city declared a state of emergency in the area, and no one was allowed back. Health officials feared an outbreak of typhoid, and the residents were forced to find temporary housing elsewhere. For a year and a half it remained an open question whether Columbia Gardens

38. *Two Goats.* 1958, 5'' and 7''.

might once again be inhabited. Finally, the city decided that until a dike was built on the banks of the Connecticut River, the area was unsafe and should be closed for residential use.

Vivolo was crushed. No matter how difficult his financial situation had been, the farm at Columbia Gardens had been a dream come true. He loved the animals, the garden, the feel of the earth, but now he would have to make a new start. The city provided little reimbursement for the condemned houses, and the residents were forced to move back to apartments in the city. Vivolo did the same, but every payday he set a dollar or two aside, hoping that one day he would again have a home of his own.

Fate had been cruel to Vivolo in the 1930's. He was not, however, a man to remain discouraged, and within two years of the heartbreaking flood, he would enjoy one of the happiest days of his life. That was the day he became an American citizen.

For Vivolo, who came to this country as an Italian immigrant, nothing seemed more important than the acquisition of his United States citizenship papers. He had always wanted to be part of the country, and to know that he had a secure place in it. He felt a strong bond

39. *Teddy Roosevelt*, 1968, 14½". Courtesy Mr. M. Tsangaris.

with his native Italy, but his real roots were in America. His children had been born and raised here, and they spoke no Italian. They were all citizens by virtue of birth, but Vivolo feared that if economic disaster struck the country and there were not enough food for all, non-citizens such as he might be deported.

He had never taken the citizenship examination for a simple and fundamental reason: he could neither read nor write. Year after year he waited, until finally his children were old enough to understand the textbook. Then they took turns drilling their father on the basic structure of American government. Who was the first American President? How many Senators were there? What branch of government was responsible for proposing new laws? What was the highest court of the land? Night after night, the children repeated the questions, and Vivolo memorized the answers meticulously.

When he arrived at the Naturalization Office, Vivolo was ready. He easily handled all of the questions fired at him by the examiners, and in no more than a matter of minutes it was all over. He had passed. He pledged allegiance to the flag and walked out an American citizen. On the way back to his apartment he had to restrain an

40. *Guitar Player*, 1970, 13½".

impulse to sing the National Anthem out loud. He took the rest of the day off from work and bought a bottle to celebrate his personal triumph.

As his children grew older and left home, much of the economic pressure which had plagued Vivolo subsided. Once again he was able to set money aside toward the purchase of land, and in 1950 he bought a site in Bloomfield and began construction of what was finally to be his permanent home. When the house was finished, Vivolo moved in with his youngest son Frank. Although he was sixty-five, no one thought of Vivolo as an old man. He could still outrun his ten year old grandson in a footrace.

THE ARTIST

He retired seven years later, and no one was surprised when he first began chiseling an old log which had been lying in the basement. Frank knew that his father needed an outlet for his energies, and he encouraged him in this pastime, never dreaming that it would develop into an all-consuming life work. Nineteen years and over one hundred and seventy pieces later, Vivolo began to achieve recognition as a folk artist.

41. Detail, *Guitar Player.*

Vivolo's work is representational, and most of his figures are of people. He refers lovingly to them as "all my wooden children." Born in his fantasy, they are molded into being by his skillful hands. He jokes with them and he treats them as members of his extended family, although declining to give any of them names. When asked why his new *Male-Female Band* (ill. 4) includes both men and women, he says he had planned to make all the musicians women, but was afraid that they would fight among themselves. Adding a few men serves to divert the women's attention and keep the peace among them.

Some of his figures look like people he has known in the past, but the resemblance is entirely coincidental. He never starts a piece with a fixed idea of how it will turn out. If one ends up looking like an old boyhood friend, Vivolo is amused. His work simply reflects his own spontaneity and love of humor. He derives great pleasure from pieces such as *Man on Black Chicken* (ill. 29).

"You ever see a man riding a chicken before?" he asks.

It is this element of surprise which makes so many of his pieces humorous.

The children themselves come in all shapes and sizes. The height of his earlier pieces ranged from fourteen to

42. *Band* detail, *Cellist*, 1969, 18". Courtesy Mr. M. Tsangaris. (See ill. 30)

eighteen inches, but some of his later figures have grown to twenty-nine and thirty-six inches. The children cover a broad spectrum of humanity, from businessmen to students, from astronauts to rock stars. Some ride animals, others play musical instruments, read books, or eat nuts and pasta. Others simply stand with outstretched arms, reaching out to touch, to be in contact. Vivolo is the source, the provider, and it is easy to visualize the wooden children marching toward him, seeking his comforting embrace. For a long time Vivolo carried the burden of rearing his large family alone; this parent-child, giving-receiving relationship has continued into his art.

It is in the painting of his figures that Vivolo's style has undergone most change. His earlier pieces were characterized by green, brown, or grey bodies, and beige faces. Pink was sometimes used to highlight such features as mustaches and hair, yet decorative detail seldom appeared. Gradually, Vivolo began experimenting with more vivid color combinations, and his work in the early 1970's was bathed in bright reds, yellows, and pinks. It was also in these pieces that Vivolo turned his attention to fine detail. Some of the nattily dressed figures come complete with sports jackets, ties, breastpocket handkerchiefs, pin-

43. Procession of carvings.

striped pants, and even shoe laces. In 1975-1976, however, less attention was being given to painting. In watching Vivolo at work, one can see why. He is now carving with such intense energy, that unfinished figures crowd his workroom. He is painting them quickly, just to get them out of the way, with the promise to return to them later.

Initially Vivolo carves the bodies of his figures roughly, using only an axe. When working on the faces, though, he is precise. He first makes a drawing on the bare wood with a compass, outlining the position of eyes, nose, and mouth. He uses the more exact tools of his trade, his chisels and files, for the face, and he often spends a whole day shaping and reshaping the expression. For him the face is the most critical part of the figure. Some of his wooden children seem surprised, others even pained, but the predominant expression is serenity. The children are peaceful, reflecting the peace which Vivolo himself has found at this stage in his life. Year after year he saw before him only an endless path of hard labor, and he never questioned his fate. But having achieved the monumental task of survival for self and family, Vivolo's struggle is over. For the first time in his life he is really the boss, his own boss, with more money in his pocket

44. *Black Man*, 1972, 14".

than he can spend. His work is not a search for a meaning in life; rather it is an expression of the joy of living. His pieces are entirely original, for he has never seen the work of another artist, has never had any training at all in art, and has never thought of himself as an artist.

Animals vie for place with human figures in his work. Simple in form, his animals come alive through the brilliant colors which he splashes on them. Horses gallop through his imaginative world in reds and pinks, goats don blue stripes, and birds stand proudly in green and yellow polka dots.

Vivolo's whirligigs are unique. They are large pieces, most of them with two or more figures, and incoporating a propeller which activates one of the figures. The propeller is often made of the top of an old five gallon can, and is connected to the moveable figure by means of a piece of heavy duty wire. The whirligigs are made for outdoors, and the propeller turns in the wind, perhaps to saw a log, perhaps to decapitate a chicken.

Some of the less intricate whirligigs are displayed on Vivolo's front lawn. Covered with objects that turn and spin, gaily painted birdhouses, stone castles, and bird baths, the lawn looks like a cross between a junkyard

45. *Speckled Chicken*, 1072, 9".

and an antiques market. But all the artifacts crowding this small space are handmade originals. Especially interesting are what Vivolo calls his "birdhouses." These are intricate stone structures which look more like igloos or the castles of storybook kings. The earliest one dates back to 1950, but some were made as recently as 1973. Built of small stones or tiles set in cement, they range in height from two to six feet.

Walking through the outside jumble of structures, the visitor arrives at the door of Vivolo's wood and brick house. Today, as always, Vivolo welcomes guests with open arms. On Sundays especially, the house is crowded with friends and relatives. Vivolo himself joins the festivities, but mainly at mealtime, for even the warmth of human companionship cannot keep him from his wooden children for long.

In his crowded workroom, standing ankle deep in sawdust, Vivolo feels at home. He lights his pipe contentedly and picks up his long rasp. It is one of his most important tools, and the wooden handle is worn smooth through years of daily use. He moves the rasp slowly across the log before him. A human face is just beginning to take shape, and Vivolo works easily, but carefully. The

40. *Castle with Conical Tower,* 1973, 56".

cycle of creation which has produced so many pieces over the last nineteen years, has begun again. Throughout his life Vivolo has always finished what he started, and this piece will be no exception. Soon it will take its place among the many children upstairs.

Watching him pour his energy into the wooden children, one believes he will simply go on forever. He is filled with so much life, so much enthusiasm, that his cautious remarks about the future seem out of place. It is easy to forget that he is at his ninetieth birthday. Suddenly the rasp stops and a mischievous look comes into Vivolo's eyes. He picks up the unfinished piece and smiles.

"You gonna play the drums, and then, if I have time...."

47. *Band* detail, *Drummer*, 1969, 16½". Courtesy Mr. M. Tsangaris. (See ill. 30)

COLOR, FORM, AND THEME [1]

When asked what kind of wood he has used for a particular piece, Vivolo shrugs. Oak, peachwood, birch, pine, whatever comes to hand serves. An oak horse may have a birch rider; a complex group may be made of pine, maple, and oak. The finished carving is sanded, treated with filler, then given an undercoat and many layers of latex. Vivolo is not enthusiastic about wood grain, and does not relish leaving a piece in its raw state. Except for a few early carvings of men emerging from

[1] Prepared by Florence Laffal

48. Unfinished pieces, 1976.

birch logs, color has always taken precedence over wood in his work.

Over the years, Vivolo's color has become brighter, and vivid patterns have appeared on the clothing of his people and in the designs adorning his animals. Although his very latest work, in 1976, shows less attention to color, this is in part because of the increased tempo of his carving. He hopes to come back to these newer pieces and give them their due in color. His first pieces were painted largely for protection against the weather, since they were meant to be exposed. In the following years he began to pay increasing attention to surface embellishment. The finished painting became at least as important as the carving itself. *Woodsman Weathervane Whirligig*, 1967 (ill. 32), is a good example of the early style. The monochromatic greens, ranging from olive drab to pale blue-green, give the work a sculptural unity that color differentiation might have marred. Such colors reflect a classical tendency found in the work of sophisticated artists, as for example, in Van Gogh, who used a palette of monochromatic browns for his early paintings of coal miners and farmers. Vivolo's greens and browns speak of the outdoors, of trees and earth reminiscent of his child-

49. *White Deer*, 1965, 18".
Courtesy Mr. M. Tsangaris.

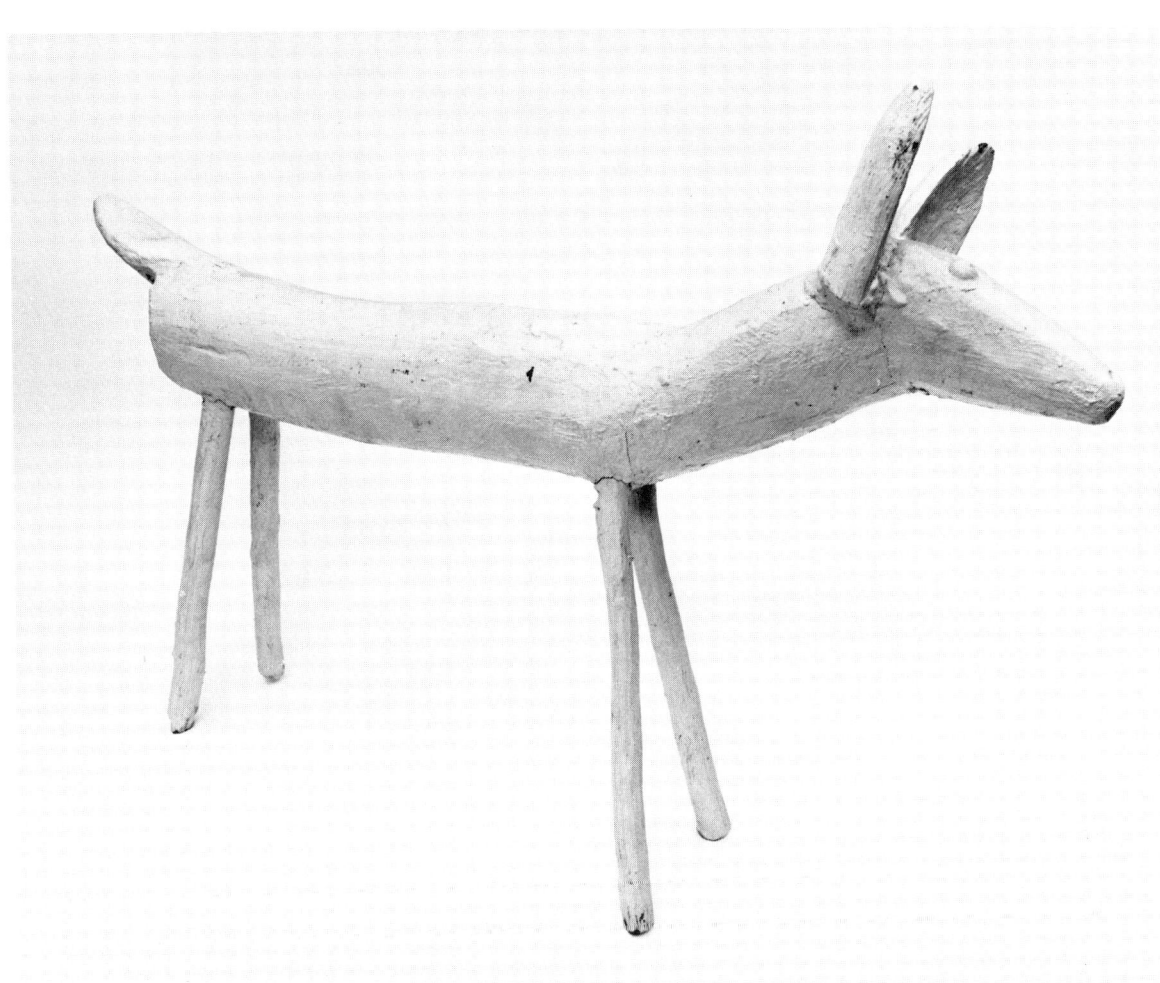

hood Italy. The weathervane whirligig is of course itself fashioned for outdoors, finding the wind direction and then exploiting it to transmit movement to the figures.

The earthy olives and browns are followed closely by pastel colors, which recur frequently throughout Vivolo's work. The cheerful *Pasta Eater* (ill. 15), with a real piece of dried spaghetti in his fork, is clothed in pale blue, and *Nutcracker Man* (ill. 59) of the same period has a pastel blue jacket. Blues of a deeper hue are given to *LBJ* (ill. 24), *Professor* (ill. 50), *Teddy Roosevelt* (ill. 39), and others of prominence. Middle range blues are thus associated with rank and station in life.

Early carvings of birds, chickens, and goats are painted off-white, with a simple one-color speckling, as in *Two Goats* (ill. 38). Quite unusual is the piece, *White Deer* (ill. 49), which is painted entirely off-white, stressing a sculptural quality. In these pieces Vivolo comes closest to presentation of the raw wood as finished product.

In the 1970's Vivolo's colors become truly brilliant, and metallic golds and silvers appear with great frequency. Color and form are now skillfully integrated, as in *Man on Black Chicken* (ill. 29). The chicken is black and its wings are suggested by swirled gold lines within which

50. *Professor*, 1964, 13½".

are red dabs with white spots. The comb is red, and the feet and beak are gold. The rider is in red, with black pants and a pointed red witch's hat. Color and design join to make a harmonious whole out of this unlikely combination. *Band* (ill. 30) has six players attired in green shirts and red pants, and two players, oddly, painted all brown. But an intuitive design sense pulls all of the musicians together in the figure of the black band leader who, much as he leads the band, combines their colors in the brown of his trousers and the red of his shirt.

In this period, without compromising his deep commitment to the carved form, Vivolo has finally abandoned himself to the joy of painting. *Rock Stars* (ill. 51) shows this delight in color. The rock star on the left has white pants, a black jacket trimmed in white, gold and black striped ascot, gold eyes, and beige hair. Not to be outdone, the second rock star wears a half-white, half-black jacket, with pockets outlined in reverse. His pants mirror-image the black and white of the jacket, and in turn, the shoes and pedestal are half-white, half-black. Magenta hair and silver eyes complete this sparkling figure.

51. *Rock Stars*, 1973, 15".

102

Although color provides a key to dating Vivolo's pieces, it does so only approximately. Early Vivolo colors recur throughout the later work, and other criteria, such as embellishment, size, and quality of the carvings must be taken into account to differentiate the periods of his work.

In 1950, at the time he was building a brick home in Bloomfield, Vivolo made a small lighthouse of cement embedded with stone and glass. The lighthouse, twenty-one inches in height, stands among the foundation plantings of the house. Since then Vivolo has constructed many masonry castles, wishing wells, and lighthouses adorned with marbles, mosaic tiles, stones, metal, and glass. Two of the numerous structures now decorating his front lawn are *Castle with Conical Tower* (ill. 46), and *Castle with Green Knob* (ill. 52). The two story *Castle with Green Knob* has fragments of pink and white ceramic tile in the roof and tower, blue doors and windows, and a tall green knob projecting high above the tower.

When Vivolo turned to wood as his major modality, his central theme became people — riding, working, playing music, smoking, or simply standing. Outstretched arms became his trademark. What do they mean? Vivolo

52 *Castle with Green Knob,*
1972, 45".

answers this question by extending his own arms and exclaiming "Come!" A favorite piece of the artist's is a large figure of a man in brown, seated with outstretched arms on a carved chair, as if both host and guest at the dinner table (ill. 27).

Vivolo draws his themes from the day to day world in which he lives, as well as from his own world of fantasy. But he does not miss out on the big world happenings. His *Astronaut* (ill. 22), clothed in a gold space suit and helmet, looks ready to board an interplanetary capsule, while *Astronaut on the Moon* (inventory 66), shows a helmeted man descending a small stairway toward a quarter moon.

When his children were growing up, Vivolo would join them in improvising on homely "instruments" to the beat of radio music. No one could match his talent on the broom, which he wedged between the door and staircase and vibrated with his hand, creating sounds akin to those of a steel brush on a drum. His carved musicians, unlike his own family group, are well equipped with instruments, percussion, string, and wind. In his nine piece *Band* (ill. 30), guitars, cello, and violin are realistically carved of wood, cymbals and traps are of metal, and

53. *Band* detail, *Traps Player,* 1969, 16½". Courtesy Mr. M. Tsangaris. (See ill. 30)

106

drums are made of small paint cans. Music is an important theme in Vivolo's work, and an in process *Male-Female Band* (ill. 4) promises to become the most complex of all his musical groupings.

It is noteworthy that the figures in Vivolo's groups, with few exceptions, do not touch each other bodily. The paradox of being part of an intimate group, yet remaining distinct as an individual, reflects Vivolo's life style. His house is overflowing with family and friends, yet he manages to spend much of his day in the solitude of his basement workshop. People are important in relation to each other, but each has his own identity and his own task to perform. *Band* (ill. 30) and *Woodsman Weathervane Whirligig* (ill. 32) show this independence of figures within a sculptural unity. One exception to this aspect of Vivolo's work is *Mother and Child* (ill. 54), a pair in which the woman holds a child in her arms. Perhaps physical contact is only for children.

The principle of physical separation is also seen in Vivolo's *Adam and Eve* (ill. 63). The bible is a source of inspiration for the work of many folk artists, and Edgar Tolson's impressive *Fall of Man* series, portraying the complete Adam and Eve saga from *Temptation* to *Expul-*

54. Mother and Child, 1970, 16". Courtesy Mr. M. Tsangaris.

sion (illustrated in Herbert W. Hemphill, Jr. and Julia Weissman, *Twentieth-Century American Folk Art and Artists*, E. P. Dutton & Co., 1974, pp. 9-21) may be compared with Vivolo's rendition. Tolson shows explicit bodily contact between Adam and Eve where Vivolo has them far apart. Nevertheless, this is the one piece in which a man and a woman are shown together. His in process *Male-Female Band* (ill. 4), when completed, will be a second work with men and women together in a group. While *Male-Female Band* will bolster the female population in Vivolo's work, there will still be no more than a dozen of them among the approximately two hundred pieces created by the artist.

Men and animals are his forte. *Cowboy on Oak Horse* (ill. 14), carved in 1958, has an uncharacteristic brown stain rubbed into the body of the horse. The horses and riders which follow become increasingly colorful, and many appurtenances are added. Some of the horses carry two riders (ill. 55). Of all his animals, the most richly decorated are his chickens and birds, and several of the chickens carry men as riders. When asked how he came to put a man on a chicken, Vivolo responds, "because he never saw such a thing." Don Quixote

55. *Horse with Two Riders,* 1974, 19".

would have welcomed any one of his chicken riders as a partner in his adventures. In the piece, *Kneeling Man on Chicken* (ill. 64), a kneeling man, reduced in size, rides a giant chicken, now elevated to a position of power and beauty. But the other side of the chicken's place in the life of man is expressed in *Chicken Slaughter Weathervane Whirligig* (ill. 56). Here the chicken lies in an unenviable position beneath the mallet of the man. A puff of wind on the sails sets the mallet in motion, and the chicken must lose its head. *Chicken Slaughter* is a work which shows the chicken in a rather undignified position. Nevertheless, colorful birds surround the hapless victim on the block and on the floor, undisturbed by the gory action, and the whole scene has a feeling not of violence, but of just another peaceful chore on a breezy day.

The most complex of all Vivolo's whirligigs is *Woodsman* (ill. 61). In it are combined themes of work, rest, and nature. If any single piece may be said to express his basic outlook, this is it. His entire life has been devoted to work: as long as one works, life goes on; to give up work is to die. Entering his ninth decade, Vivolo feels an urgency to complete his work. Like the woodsman, he

56. Detail, *Chicken Slaughter Weathervane Whirligig*, 1966, 20"x17"x15½". Courtesy Kelter-Malce. (See ill. 19)

must keep at it constantly, driven by natural forces within, as the arm of the woodsman is driven by the wind. But afterward, as one of the figures in the whirligig suggests, there is rest, and one may smoke one's pipe in peace, knowing he has done an honest day's or an honest lifetime's work. The best place of all for work or rest is outdoors, in the summer sun, a bird perched on a shoulder, feet planted on the soil.

Flag Weathervane Whirligig (ill. 35), made in 1975, expresses a bicentennial theme of celebration. In it, the eighty-nine year old Italian-American artist creates a light-hearted fantasy honoring the two hundredth birthday of his adopted land. It is painted in brilliant greens, blues, pinks, and reds. A standing figure rocks forward and back as the wind activates the rotary sails, and his saw cuts an upright log. A seated man, perched nearby in a tree, rotates slightly as the pinwheel in his hand catches the wind. An early American flag rides high above all. Its two-dimensionality and the fanciful figure on his precarious perch, give the *Flag Whirligig* an airy look, as though with the greatest of ease it could sail off into the sky.

57. Detail, *Woodsman Weathervane Whirligig*, 1967, 12½".
Courtesy Mr. & Mrs. J. Laffal.
(See ill. 32, 61)

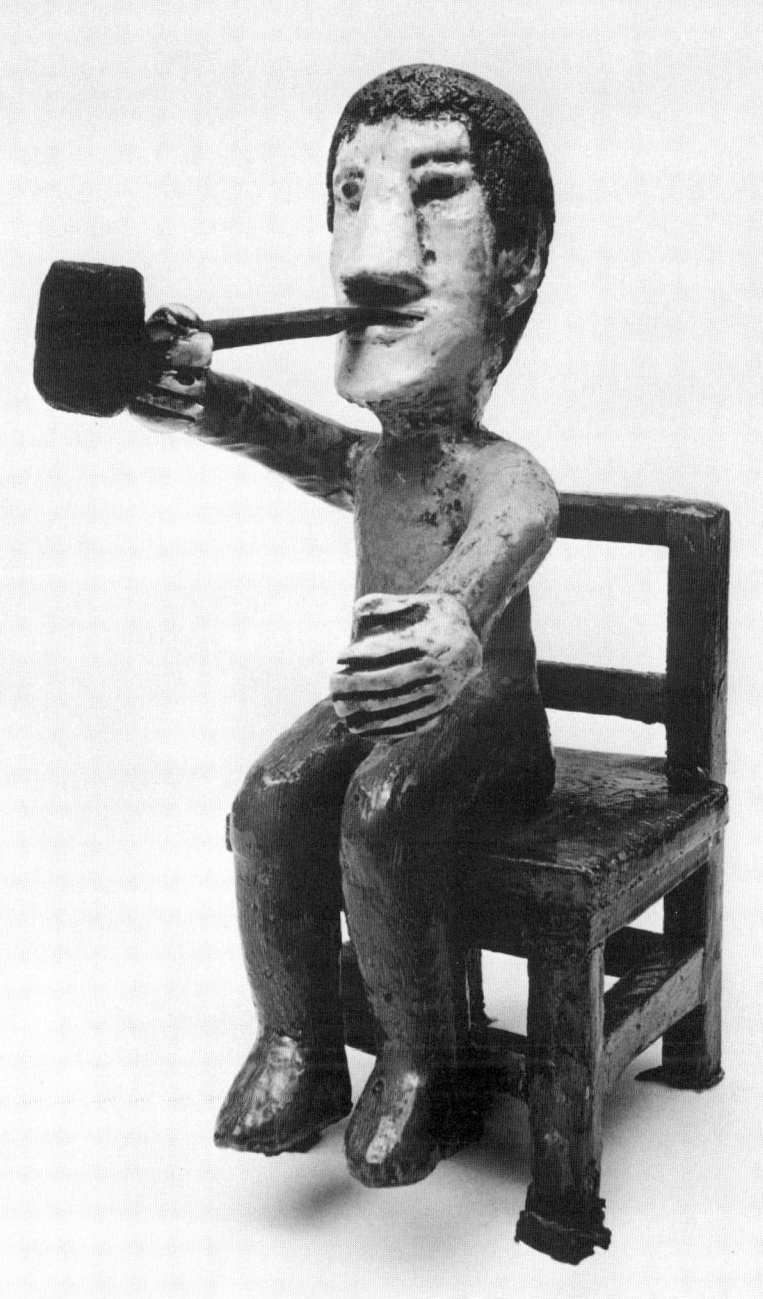

58. *Red Horse*, 1974. Height 16½", length 21". Red latex.

Wishing to make a giraffe, Vivolo chipped away at a log until an elongated animal took shape. At this point he realized that his image of a giraffe was not precise, so he asked his grandson to bring him a picture of the animal from the Public Library. Characteristically impatient, when the picture was not immediately forthcoming, he shortened the neck of the figure, made a few other alterations, and the giraffe became a horse. It is one of the few horses of its kind in his work, painted solid red with no embellishments whatever. The long-necked linear animal evokes comparison with the wood horse of Marino Marini's 1953 *Horse and Rider.*

59. *Nutcracker Man*, 1963. Height 13″.
Black and blue latex.

The *Nutcracker Man* waits for someone to
put a nut in his mouth from the tray in
his lap. First Vivolo carves his figure of a
man, then he cuts out the lower jaw from
chin to mouth, as well as a square hole
through the back of the neck. A new chin
with handle protruding through the neck
hole becomes the moveable lower jaw of
the nutcracker, pivoting on a pin through
the side of the neck. A spring holds the
handle to a nail in the back of the figure
and returns the man's jaw to its resting
position after use. *Nutcracker Man* actually cracks nuts.

60. *Candle Man*, 1970. Height 13½". Red, gold, and black latex.

Named *Candle Man* because of the "wick" protruding from the top of his hat, this figure is typical of Vivolo's brilliantly colored pieces of early 1970. The shirt is red, with gold speckling and bands, and the pants are red, with black stripes. The hat is gold, with a black band, and the shoes are white. The figure stands with arms extended in the familiar Vivolo "Come" posture. The bent nail "wick" actually serves a practical purpose, and many of the artist's pieces have a bent nail, usually in some less obvious place. Pieces are hung up by the nail for final painting and drying, and the artist sometimes neglects to pull the nail out afterward.

61. *Woodsman Weathervane Whirligig,*
1967. Height 38″, length 37″. Olive green,
brown, and blue green latex. Courtesy
Mr. & Mrs. J. Laffal. (See ill. 32, 57, 62)

Woodsman Weathervane Whirligig has a
complex theme of nature, work, and rest.
This piece, more fully than any other, expresses Vivolo's philosophy of unity with,
and acceptance of, the world of nature
and of man. As nature, by its seasons and
its changes, sets all in motion, so man, by
his vital power and his work, creates and
builds. And when work is over, a man
can light up his pipe and feel at rest,
ready to offer an open welcome to others
as well. A large figure with saw in right
hand, axe in left, dwarfs the three smaller
figures. As the windmill revolves in the
breeze, the woodsman saws a log. The
other figures are stationary: a seated man
calmly smokes a pipe, and two others
stand with arms extended in typical
Vivolo pose. A small bird is perched on
the shoulder of the standing man, and a
large bird sits on the post of the windmill. Colors of earth and vegetation pre-
dominate.

62. Detail, *Woodsman Weathervane Whirligig*. (See ill. 32, 61)

The principle by which movement is imparted in Vivolo's weathervane whirligigs is shown in this picture. The striped directional vane in the upper left, made of wood, rotates the whole whirligig so that the wind blows directly into the rotary sail. The rotary sail is made by cutting and bending sections in the cover of a five gallon utility can. As the sail revolves, the projecting pin, slightly off center, undergoes a circular movement, and the wire attached to this pin and the man's saw hand, raises and lowers the man's arm. The arm is pivoted at the shoulder, and the saw itself is loose, so that the up and down movement conveys a forward and back motion to the saw. The man's axe arm remains rigid. The plate over the woodsman's pivoting shoulder, adorned by a bird, serves as a water run-off and protection against the weather, so that this crucial joint does not rust into immobility in the out-of-doors where the piece is meant to be. A similar plate behind the rotary sail, not visible in this picture, protects the joint between the sail and its wood supporting post. The wire hanging beneath the rotary sail is a hook on which an oil can may be hung for lubricating the whirligig.

63. *Adam and Eve*, 1975. Height, figures 14", tree 19". Pink, green, red, and brown latex.

Adam and Eve is an unusual theme for Vivolo who is not inclined toward religious or biblical depiction. However, the theme is characteristically found in the work of folk artists. Two pink figures face a tree made of twisted wire painted brown. Green leaves and red apples are fashioned from wood filler and glue. Adam reaches to pluck an apple while the black serpent, wound about the trunk of the tree, observes.

64. *Kneeling Man on Chicken*, 1976.
Height 24", length 22". Brown, green,
red, and white latex.

A kneeling man rides a giant, long-legged
chicken. This is Vivolo's largest carving in
the "man on a chicken" theme. The
chicken is in brick color, with black spots.
The kneeling man has a brown suit and
brown hat, with green brim. Vivolo put a
man on a chicken because, as he says, he
never saw such a thing in real life. However, the chicken does, in real life, support
the man as much as the horse does its
rider, namely, by providing him with food.
Vivolo is not explicit about this idea, but
his lifelong struggle to provide food and
and shelter for his family, leads to such a
suggestion.

65. *Flag Weathervane Whirligig*, 1975.
Height, 31'', length, 44''. Green, red,
white, and blue latex. (See ill. 35, 36)

Flag Whirligig has a complicated set of
actions. The wind activates the large windmill, and the standing man rocks forward
and back as the saw, held by a pin between his hands, moves to saw a log. In-
dependently, the other man, seated atop a
tree branch, rotates slightly as the wind
catches the pinwheel in his hand. Vivolo's
feeling for design is clearly manifested in
this piece. Overall the design is linear,
with all parts fitted into an off-center
triangle. The lowest point of the triangle
is the circular sail of the windmill. From
there the eye is carried to the standing
man with the saw, then on to the seated
man, and to the apex — the flag — then
back down, finally, to the vane. The piece
has a pop art quality enhanced by its
vivid colors and early American flag riding
high over all, reflecting a bicentennial
motif. The standing man has a tall bright
green pointed hat matching his own pants
and the suit of the seated figure. The
seated man has a dark green flat hat, the
color of the wood-sawer's jacket, the tree
branch, and the base. A vivid blue star
decorates the red vane, and the same
highly contrasting colors are on the vanes
of the circular windmill sail.

INVENTORY

Included in the inventory are all of Vivolo's finished pieces known to exist as of April 10, 1976. Pieces are listed under major subject headings, by title, date, height (and length in some cases), distinctive features, owner unless owned by the artist himself or his family, and illustration number if pictured in the book.

Animals

1. *Black Bird*, 1958, 8". Black, red breast, white tail and wings.
2. *Black Bird*, 1969, 4". Black with pink dots.
3. *Black Bird*, 1975, 10". Black, brown and gold wings, red tail with brown stripes, silver eyes.
4. *Bluebird on Birdhouse*, 1969, 12". Bluebird on roof of white birdhouse. diCorcia/Zuber, Boston.
5. *Green Bird*, 1970, 4½". Green with red wings, gold head, red dots on body.
6. *Green Bird*, 1970, 6½". Green with black dots, pink eyes.
7. *Pink Bird*, 1971, 6". Pink and red; white and black tail (ill. 31).
8. *Red Bird*, 1960, 6". Red with gold beak, vari-colored dots.
9. *Red Bird*, 1970, 7". Red with green wings and tail, black dots on back.
10. *Silver Bird*, 1974, 10". Silver with red crest and brown spots. Mr. M. Tsangaris, New York.
11. *Speckled Bird*, 1970, 9½". Speckled green and white. Mr. M. Tsangaris, New York.
12. *Speckled Bird*, 1972, 7". Speckled white and green; red and white speckled beak (ill. 31).
13. *Speckled Bird*, 1973, 7". Violet with white dots; green and red stripes (ill. 31).
14. *Speckled Bird*, 1974, 6". Silver, black, and red.
15. *Speckled Bird*, 1975, 8". Black with white and green specks.
16. *Spotted Bird*, 1970, 6½". Spotted red, with pink eyes.

17. *Tan Bird*, 1956, 3″. Tan with carved wings.
18. *Tan Bird*, 1957, 3″. Black and tan with green spots.
19. *White Bird*, 1970, 5½″. White with brown eyes; smiling. diCorcia/Zuber, Boston.
20. *White Bird*, 1974, 10″. White with brown beak, brown bands and spots. Mr. M. Tsangaris, New York.
21. *White Bird*, 1974, 9½″. White with brown eyes and brown legs. Mr. M. Tsangaris, New York.
22. *Gold Chicken*, 1974, 5½″. Gold, red, green, and white, with bent nail "worm" in beak.
23. *Red Chicken*, 1974, 6½″. Red with blue spots.
24. *Speckled Chicken*, 1972, 9″. White with brown specks and brown comb (ill. 45).
25. *Blue Deer*, 1975, 29½″. Log body, tree branch legs. Mr. M. Tsangaris, New York.
26. *Gold Deer*, 1974, 28″. Gold with black hooves.
27. *Gold Deer*, 1974, 28″. Gold with black hooves.
28. *Gold Deer*, 1974, 28″. Gold with black hooves.
29. *White Deer*, 1965, 18″. Log body, tree branch legs. Mr. M. Tsangaris, New York (ill. 49).
30. *White Deer*, 1970, 19″. Log body, tree branch legs. Kelter-Malce, New York.
31. *Black Dog*, 1973, 6½″. All black.
32. *Green Dog*, 1962, 7″. All green.
33. *Lamb Dog*, 1971, 13½″. Grey curly hair; brown feet, nose, and eyes. Mr. M. Tsangaris, New York (ill. 18).
34. *White Dog*, 1970, 12″. White with brown splotches; brown marble eyes. diCorcia/Zuber, Boston.
35. *White Dog*, 1971, 10″. White with marble eyes. diCorcia/Zuber, Boston.
36. *Goat*, 1958, 5″. White with blue stripes (ill. 38).
37. *Goat*, 1958, 7″. White with blue dots (ill. 38).
38. *Black Horse*, 1963, 9″. All black.
39. *Red Horse*, 1974, 16½″. All red; elongated neck (ill. 58).
40. *Zebra*, 1956, 9½″. Blue with white stripes.
41. *Zebra*, 1958, 8½″. Blue with white stripes.

Animals and Riders

42. *Kneeling Man on Chicken*, 1976, 24″. Giant chicken in brick red with black spots, man has brown suit (ill. 64).
43. *Man on Black Chicken*, 1974, 18″. Chicken is black, gold, and red, man has pointed red hat. Mr. & Mrs. J. Laffal, Essex, Conn. (ill. 29).
44. *Man on White-tailed Chicken*, 1974, 18″. White-tailed chicken, man with white hat sits on chicken's neck (ill. 20).
45. *Man on Green Chicken*, 1976, 15″. Green chicken, gold spots.
46. *Cowboy on Horse*, 1958, 18″. Bronze horse, white-hatted rider.
47. *Cowboy on Horse*, 1972, 14½″. Brown horse, white tail.
48. *Cowboy on Horse*, 1974, 18″. Pink horse, cowboy with guitar, fur jacket, white hat (ill 23).
49. *Cowboy on Oak Horse*, 1958, 18″. Brown stained horse, man holds pistol (ill. 14).
50. *Horse and Rider*, 1956, 11″. Horse has white stripes on face.
51. *Horse and Rider*, 1957, 13″. Red horse, rider holds gun.
52. *Horse and Rider*, 1970, 12″. Black horse, silver saddle.
53. *Horse and Rider*, 1971, 22″. Horse has white mane, tail, ankles.
54. *Horse with Two Riders*, 1974, 19″. Forward rider has black shirt and red hat, rear rider has pink shirt and brown hat (ill. 55).
55. *Horse with Two Riders*, 1974, 19″. "Father and son" riders, son kneeling on horse's haunches. Mr. M. Tsangaris, New York.
56. *Indian on Silver Horse*, 1959, 9″. Silver horse with blue spots, Indian with feathers. diCorcia/Zuber, Boston.
57. *Man on Pony*, 1970, 9½″. Pony has white mane and feet.

Masonry Structures

58. *Castle*, 1972, 26½″. Cement with embedded stone, metal, tile.
59. *Castle with Balcony*, 1972, 32″. Cement, with window.
60. *Castle with Conical Tower*, 1973, 56″. Cement, with window, "witch's hat" tower, stone insets (ill. 46).

61. *Castle with Green Knob*, 1972, 45". Cement and colored
    tiles, blue door and window, green knob above all (ill. 52).
62. *Castle with Square Top*, 1973, 34". Cement, with window.
63. *Lighthouse*, 1950, 21". Cement with stones, marbles, beads.
64. *Man on Tower*, 1966, 38". Wood man smoking pipe on cement
    tower decorated with stone and glass. diCorcia/Zuber, Boston.

Men

65. *Astronaut,* 1971, 13". Gold with black decorations, pointed
    helmet, raised visor (ill. 22).
66. *Astronaut on the Moon*, 1971, 17". Astronaut with helmet is
    ready to descend stairway to quarter moon.
67. *Astronaut on the Moon*, 1971, 17". Similar to 66.
68. *Black Man*, 1972, 14". Black man in white suit and hat (ill. 44).
69. *Candle Man*, 1970, 13½". Speckled gold shirt, gold hat with
    bent nail "candle wick" (ill. 60).
70. *Devil*, 1969, 14". Brown devil with horns and serpent tail.
    Mr. M. Tsangaris, New York (ill. 21).
71. *Emerging Man*, 1958, 14". Bust of man on wood stump. Gold
    with flesh colored face and hands.
72. *Emerging Man*, 1969, 6½". See 71. White stripes on yellow face.
73. *Emerging Man*, 1971, 9". See 71. Grey hair.
74. *Emerging Man*, 1974, 29½". Bronze hair and mustache, white
    base. Made of fence post. Mr. M. Tsangaris, New York.
75. *Farmer with Pitchfork*, 1966, 24". Farmer holds metal pitch-
    fork. Mr. & Mrs. M. Cappetta, S. J. Capistrano, Calif.
76. *Guitar Player*, 1970, 13½". Gold hair, four string guitar
    (ill. 40, 41).
77. *Indian*, 1958, 9". Bust only, red hat with feather, blue jacket.
78. *Indian*, 1958, 10". Kneeling, drawing bow, single feather.
79. *Indian*, 1958, 11". Seated on birch throne, with steel arrows.
80. *Indian*, 1959, 9". Drawn bow and arrow, red-tipped arrows in
    quiver. Mr. M. Tsangaris, New York.
81. *Jockey*, 1958, 10". Red cap, yellow pants.

82. *Kneeling Man with Rifle*, 1968, 8½". Green shirt, red pants.
83. *Lantern Man*, 1960, 13". Standing man holding lantern, white shirt, striped sleeves, gold hat.
84. *Lantern Man*, 1961, 11". See 83. All beige (ill. 12).
85. *Lantern Man*, 1967, 15". See 83. Brown suit. Kelter-Malce, New York.
86. *Lantern Man*, 1969, 16". See 83. Black man with red pants. diCorcia/Zuber, Boston.
87. *Lantern Man*, 1970, 20½". See 83. Generally pink, green hair.
88. *Lantern Man*, 1975, 36". Man stands on brown stump; blue shirt, brown pants (ill. 12).
89. *Lantern Man*, 1976, 22". See 83. Green shirt, black pants.
90. *Lantern Man*, 1976, 21". See 83. Blue shirt, black pants.
91. *LBJ*, 1968, 14". Detachable metal hat, blue shirt, wire spectacles. Mr. M. Tsangaris, New York (ill. 24, 25).
92. *Man and Child*, 1967, 12". Man holds 4" child on his hand. Green and blue. diCorcia/Zuber, Boston.
93. *Man on a Chair*, 1975, 36". Brown suit, carved chair (ill. 8, 27).
94. *Nutcracker Man*, 1963, 13". Man's jaw cracks nuts. Blue clothes, black hair (ill. 59).
95. *Nutcracker Man*, 1965, 16½". See 94. Green pants, silver shoes. Mr. & Mrs. M. Cappetta, S. J. Capistrano, Calif.
96. *Nutcracker Man*, 1971, 14". See 94. Blue jacket, yellow pants. Mr. A. Zuccaro, Bolton, Conn.
97. *Nutcracker Man*, 1971, 14½". See 94. Generally blue, gold hair. Mr. A. Zuccaro, Bolton, Conn.
98. *Nutcracker Man*, 1971, 16". See 94. Generally blue, gold hair.
99. *Nutcracker Man*, 1974, 16". See 94. Blue jacket, yellow pants. Mr. M. Tsangaris, New York.
100. *Nutcracker Man*, 1976, 19½". See 94. Black hair, gold hat.
101. *Nutcracker Man*, 1976, 20". See 94. Black hat and mustache (ill. 34).
102. *Pasta Eater*, 1971, 21½". Man with bowl and raised fork with spaghetti. Mr. M. Tsangaris, New York (ill. 15, 16).

103. *Production Boss*, 1958, 16". Visor cap, steel grey spectacles, blue jacket (ill. 26).
104. *Professor*, 1964, 13½". Man with spectacles, book, removable metal hat (ill. 50).
105. *Rock Star*, 1973, 15". White pants, black jacket (ill. 51).
106. *Rock Star*, 1973, 15". Clothing half-black, half-white (ill. 51).

Standing Men:
107. 1960, 17½". Generally green, with blonde hair and mustache.
108. 1960, 11". Maroon and black, with cream shirt.
109. 1960, 10". Red cap, blue jacket, green pants.
110. 1964, 13½". Raspberry hair, gold clothing.
111. 1965, 15½". Generally red, beige hair.
112. 1965, 16½". Brown pants, brown shirt with white dots.
113. 1966, 12½". Grey pants, blue jacket. Mr. & Mrs. M. Cappetta, S. J. Capistrano, Calif.
114. 1966, 6½". Green pants, blue shirt, copper hat. Mr. & Mrs. M. Cappetta, S. J. Capistrano, Calif.
115. 1967, 17½". Blue jacket, grey hair. Kelter-Malce, New York.
116. 1968, 14". Strawberry hair, gold face, black pants.
117. 1968, 18". Green clothing, cream hair and mustache.
118. 1968, 14". All pink, with black dot eyes.
119. 1968, 10½". Gold hair, gold suit with dots.
120. 1969, 15". Green jacket, gold ascot. Kelter-Malce, New York.
121. 1969, 17½". Blue jacket, gold ascot. Kelter-Malce, New York.
122. 1969, 9". Aqua shirt, fedora with red band. diCorcia/Zuber, Boston.
123. 1970, 20". Pink shirt, blue pants, black hair.
124. 1970, 16". Red shirt, brown pants, gold shoes, gold hair.
125. 1970, 17". Red shirt outlined in white, brown hair.
126. 1970, 12½". Red bordered black shirt, silver pants, gold hair.
127. 1970, 15". Pink suit, cream hair, gold eyes.
128. 1970, 16". Green suit, tan hair.
129. 1971, 17½". Lavender hair. Kelter-Malce, New York.
130. 1971, 9". Red pants, silver shirt trimmed in black, gold hair.

131. 1972, 14″. Red shirt, black pants, pink shoes, grey hair.
132. 1972, 15½″. Red clothing, tan hair.
133. 1973, 14″. Red jacket, pink pants, rust hair.
134. 1973, 14″. Pink shirt, gold pants, black hair.
135. 1974, 15″. Red shirt with black dots, grey pants, black hair.
136. 1974, 19½″. Blue shirt, blue-green pants, green jacket. Mr. M. Tsangaris, New York.
137. 1975, 14″. Brown shirt, white pants, black hair.
138. 1975, 16″. Black clothing, green hands, beige hair.
139. 1976, 21½″. Brown pants, green shirt, yellow hair.
140. 1976, 24″. Brown clothing, brick red pointed hat and hair.
141. 1976, 26″. Brown clothing, brick red hat and hair.
142. 1976, 21″. Brown shirt, green pants, steel grey hair.
143. 1976, 16″. Green clothing, beige hair.
144. 1976, 19″. Brown clothing, buff hair.
145. 1976, 16½″. Bottle green clothing, grey hair.
146. 1976, 17″. Bottle green clothing, black hair.
147. 1976, 19″. Green shirt, beige pants, beige hair.
148. 1976, 16″. Green shirt, brown pants, grey hair and mustache.
149. 1976, 29½″. Black mustached, black hair and derby, green shirt (ill. 17).
150. 1976, 19½″. Pale green suit, beige hair and mustache.
151. 1976, 14″. Brown suit, white shirt and tie.

152. *Teddy Roosevelt*, 1968, 14½″. Seated in birch trunk, reads wood book. Mr. M. Tsangaris, New York (ill. 39).
153. *Telescope Man*, 1974, 12″. Man has telescope in one hand, lantern in other. Ms. J. Whritner, Brooklyn, N. Y.
154. *Viola Player*, 1966, 15½″. Man has detachable viola. Grey clothing. Mr. & Mrs. M. Cappetta, S. J. Capistrano, Calif.

Women

155. *Female Guitarist*, 1966, 13½″. Blue tunic, silver boots, removable guitar. Mr. & Mrs. M. Cappetta, S. J. Capistrano, Calif.
156. *Gold Lady*, 1973, 14½″. Gold clothing, magenta hair (ill. 37).

157. *Mother and Child*, 1970, 16". Woman holds detachable child. Mr. M. Tsangaris, New York (ill. 54).
158. *Standing Woman*, 1970, 11". Brown blouse, long green skirt.
159. *Woman with Baby*, 1976, 19½". Blue Blouse, brown skirt, plastic bird on woman's head. Baby is 9".
160. *Wonder Woman*, 1966, 12". Dull gold hair, dress made of Wonder Bread wrapper. Mr. M. Tsangaris, New York (ill. 13).

Weathervane Whirligigs and Groups of Figures

161. *Adam and Eve*, 1975, 19". Naked pink man and woman, black snake in apple tree (ill. 63).
162. *Airplane Weathervane*, 1969, 12"x27". Turquoise airplane of auto and paint can parts. Mr. M. Tsangaris, New York.
163. *Band*, 1969, 16½" to 18". Nine musicians. Two guitars, cello, violin, drummer, clarinet, in green shirts and red pants. Cymbals, traps, in brown. Black band leader in red shirt and brown pants. Mr. M. Tsangaris, New York (ill. 30, 42, 47, 53).
164. *Barbershop Trio*, 1973, 15". Three male singers in striped and speckled jackets, ascots, heavily outlined eyes (ill. 33).
165. *Chicken Chopper Weathervane Whirligig*, 1975, 22"x38". As windmill turns, axe in man's right hand and chicken in his left hand, fall on the block together.
166. *Chicken Slaughter Weathervane Whirligig*, 1966, 20"x17"x15½". As windmill turns, mallet in man's hand comes down on chicken's head. Other birds nearby are gold and blue. Man has red hat, gold hair. Kelter-Malce, New York (ill. 19, 56).
167. *Flag Weathervane Whirligig*, 1975, 31"x44". As windmill turns, man saws log. Smaller figure with pinwheel also turns. Early American flag tops all. Colors are green, red, blue (ill. 35, 36, 65).
168. *Log Sawer Weathervane Whirligig*, 1967, 17"x41". As windmill turns, man saws wood. Man has brown hair, green hands. Kelter-Malce, New York.

169. *Man Chopping Wood Weathervane Whirligig*, 1970, 12''x31''. As windmill turns, man chops wood. Mr. M. Tsangaris, New York.

170. *Meeting*, 1973, 7'' to 8''. Four truncated figures in brown clothing, grey bearded leader with book (ill. 11).

171. *Sawing Wood Weathervane Whirligig*, 1971, 13''. As windmill turns, man saws wood. Red donkey nearby. Man has red vest, green pants. Mr. A. Zuccaro, Bolton, Conn.

172. *Sawing Wood Weathervane Whirligig*, 1975, 19''x46''. As windmill turns, man saws wood (ill. 10).

173. *Woodsman Weathervane Whirligig*, 1967, 38''x37''. As windmill turns, one man saws wood, three other men nearby — one seated with pipe. Two birds. Olive drab, blue-green, and brown. Mr. & Mrs. J. Laffal, Essex, Conn. (ill. 32, 57, 61, 62).

In Process

174. *Male-Female Band*, 1976 (ill. 4).

CHRONOLOGY

1950. Masonry *Lighthouse.*

1956. *Tan Bird, Zebra, Horse and Rider.*

1957. *Tan Bird, Horse and Rider.*

1958. *Black Bird,* 2 *Goats, Zebra, Cowboy on Horse, Cowboy on Oak Horse, Emerging Man,* 3 *Indians, Jockey, Production Boss.*

1959. *Indian on Silver Horse, Indian.*

1960. *Red Bird, Lantern Man,* 3 *Standing Men.*

1961. *Lantern Man.*

1962. *Green Dog.*

1963. *Black Horse, Nutcracker Man.*

1964. *Professor, Standing Man.*

1965. *White Deer, Nutcracker Man,* 2 *Standing Men.*

1966. *Farmer with Pitchfork, Man on Tower,* 2 *Standing Men, Viola Player, Female Guitarist, Wonder Woman, Chicken Slaughter Weathervane Whirligig.*

1967. *Lantern Man, Man and Child, Standing Man, Log Sawer Weathervane Whirligig, Woodsman Weathervane Whirligig.*

1968. *Kneeling Man with Rifle, LBJ,* 4 *Standing Men, Teddy Roosevelt.*

1969. *Black Bird, Bluebird on Birdhouse, Devil, Emerging Man, Lantern Man,* 3 *Standing Men, Airplane Weathervane, Band* (9 pieces).

1970. 6 *Birds, White Deer, White Dog, Horse and Rider, Man on Pony, Candle Man, Guitar Player, Lantern Man,* 6 *Standing Men, Mother and Child, Standing Woman, Man Chopping Wood Weathervane Whirligig.*

1971. *Pink Bird, Lamb Dog, White Dog, Horse and Rider, Astronaut,* 2 *Astronauts on the Moon, Emerging Man,* 3 *Nutcracker Men, Pasta Eater,* 2 *Standing Men, Sawing Wood Weathervane Whirligig.*

1972. *Speckled Bird, Chicken, Cowboy on Horse,* 3 masonry *Castles, Black Man,* 2 *Standing Men.*

1973. *Speckled Bird, Black Dog,* 2 masonry *Castles,* 2 *Rock Stars,* 2 *Standing Men, Gold Lady, Barbershop Trio, Meeting* (4 figures).

1974. 4 *Birds,* 2 *Chickens,* 3 *Deer, Red Horse, Man on Black Chicken, Man on White-tailed Chicken, Cowboy on Horse,* 2 *Horses with Two Riders, Emerging Man, Nutcracker Man,* 2 *Standing Men, Telescope Man.*

1975. 2 *Birds, Blue Deer, Lantern Man, Man on a Chair,* 2 *Standing Men, Adam and Eve, Chicken Chopper Weathervane Whirligig, Flag Weathervane Whirligig, Sawing Wood Weathervane Whirligig.*

1976. *Kneeling Man on Chicken, Man on Green Chicken,* 2 *Lantern Men,* 2 *Nutcracker Men,* 13 *Standing Men, Woman with Baby.*

In process: *Male-Female Band.*

ACKNOWLEDGMENTS

Gallery Press wishes to express appreciation to those who provided material for *Vivolo and His Wooden Children*, and made its publication possible. Frank Vivolo helped immeasurably in locating and dating his father's work, and his wife Marilyn, and sister Jean Marashiello, were gracious hosts to the author, Ken Laffal, in his many visits to the Vivolo home.

The following collectors of Vivolo work willingly provided detailed information about the Vivolo pieces in their possession or in the possession of others: Michael Tsangaris, Kelter-Malce Gallery, diCorcia/Zuber, Mr. and Mrs. Michael Cappetta, Albert Zuccaro, and Mr. and Mrs. Julius Laffal.

Dee Burghardt, reporter for the *New Haven Register* kindly permitted use of her photographs of Vivolo and his work which appear on pages 19, 20, 27, and 30.

The quotation on page 13, from *Twentieth-Century American Folk Art and Artists* by Herbert W. Hemphill Jr. and Julia Weissman, first published in 1974, is reprinted with the permission of E. P. Dutton & Co., Inc., all rights reserved.